In the Arc Welder's Blinding Light

In the Arc Welder's Blinding Light

John B. Lee

First Edition

 Wet Ink Books
www.WetInkBooks.com
WetInkBooks@gmail.com

In the Arc Welder's Blinding Light
by John B. Lee

Cover Design – Richard M. Grove
Layout and Design – Richard M. Grove
Cover Image – Richard M. Grove

Typeset in Garamond
Printed and bound in Canada
Distributed in USA by Ingram,
– to set up an account – 1-800-937-0152

Library and Archives Canada Cataloguing in Publication

Title: In the arc welder's blinding light / John B. Lee.
Names: Lee, John B., 1951- author.
Description: Poems.
Identifiers: Canadiana 20220398585 | ISBN 9781989786741 (softcover)
Classification: LCC PS8573.E348 I5144 2022 | DDC C811/.54—dc23

Previously Published

... *poems from* In the Arc Welder's Blinding Light *have been published in* Literature for the People, *Issue No. 2,* Lummox Number nine, Love Lies Bleeding, The Banister Volume 36, The Banister Volume 37, Dancing on Stones *anthology, and* Phantom Parade *anthology*

the title poem "In the Arc Welder's Blinding Light," received first prize in the Banister Poetry Awards 2021

"Unimportant Work" received Honourable Mention in the 2021 Banister poetry awards

"The Carpenter's Apprentice," won 3rd place in the 2022 Banister poetry awards

"The Milkman's Epiphany," received an Honourable Mention in the 2022 Love Lies Bleeding anthology

"Like Wordsworth I Find Myself Composing as I Walk," "The Rope Maker's Imaginings," and "The Watchmaker's Darkness," appeared in the chapbook My Sister Rides a Sorrow Mule *winner of the Golden Grassroots Chapbook Award (Beret Days Book)*

for my ancestors,
and for all the elder knowledge we have lost

and most especially for my maternal grandmother, Lila Busteed nee Woofenden,
born at the turn of the century in the age of horses, and who lived through the
advent of the automobile, the first flight of the Wright brothers at Kitty
Hawk, and from then through to the first great war, the 1918 influenza
epidemic, the Great Depression, World War Two, the splitting of the atom,
and the dropping of the atomic bomb on Hiroshima and Nagasaki, the landing
of a man on the moon, and from then well into the computer age, and for what
she might remember and what she might imagine, living her last years in a
retirement home where well into the decline of old age, the dear old blind lady,
whenever she was asked 'How are you today, grandma?' would respond 'I just
count my blessings" — and for that heroic example I will always remain truly
grateful ...

.... well as for me, I was born taking my first breath in the eternal and ever-
present peril of total annihilation from thermo-nuclear war. According to my
mother, my first words were "Howdy Doody" and my final words, at least for
now, "I don't know what that means ..."

table of content

Whisper these words ...

*be the breeze that breaks the branch
from the tree no longer there*

.

That First Winter

what must it have been like
that first winter
in the boreal and
swampy wilderness
when every chink and hollow
in the lean-to shelter
was weather worried
living in a land
so raw with stumps
and slashes
near the shadow thicket
of a wolf-thick woods
oh my ancestor Irish
with your faith in summer
starving at the root
and the snowfall
thriving like the crystal seed
of midnight moons
while the deer buck
dropping his rack
cracked saplings
for the want of green
and coyotes slaked their tongues on ice
and then the nearby loosening lake
released the broken mirror
as it rose a shattered image
crashing on the grey-blue
iconoclasm of the heaven-smashing shore

what warms
the snake and makes
life supple in the knoll
or pulls a living thread
through softening clay
makes water witches
of a widow's hands
and wells within the arrow
of the drooping branch
cathedrals in the oriole-nesting oak
and garden in the scree
and weed

go wake the dead remainder
of a lingering frost
the thinning away
of a shining hoar
what wilts
then lifts its blossoming branches
to the sun
makes quick the axe
and speeds the saw
the larder swollen and
the cold frame full – mosquito choirs
sing in canticles of celebrated heat
and flies that nip
a crimson shoulder
quicken work

go seek the buried bones
of ancient beasts
and from that fertile absence
find the flint
that shapes the grave

imagine time
within a single man
the milken stars of him
gone dry with day
while death-pierced generations
fall like fruit crops
in the come and go of life
what feeds the heart
when pleasure shocks the loins
to slake a thirst
or fill the breast with breath
the common mind
of cave and cabin
the grotto or the gabled house
in hardship and in ease
construct the leisure of a loving thought
that's also troubled by eventual loss

The Watchmaker's Darkness

imagine you are a boy of five
living in coal country
in nineteenth century England
and you are lowered
without light or candle
into the bowels of the earth
standing small
in the unambiguous black
at the place
where the darkness
touches the wall
and you are there
twelve hours blind
like an ogre's child
in the water clock
of a rich man's mine
six years dripping
as you crouch at the coal face
standing like a cold door
close as night
to death and death
to dust
and the lost skill
of breathing
the bituminous taste of blackening air
how steam and all
the awful machinery
of iron-boned earth
comes clamouring out of the grave
as though
time were not measured
in crimson gloaming

and thunder at midnight comes early
and again in the comes-late dawn
what's life but a joyless rumour
groaning in a broken shambles
with thin shoulders in rags
and small hands
clutching a rope

An Ode to Rock Russell –
the last blacksmith in the village

the last living blacksmith in the village
was already
an anachronism by the time I was born
his sad obsolescence obvious to all
in the somnolent hour of the fading away
of the purpose of horses at work
their harnesses
hung on the breath of the wall
in the barns of the farm
the leather gone green as grass-eating tongues
the collar that yoked them
circled in mould like a dusting of sugar on dough
and even his name
spoke of fustian smoke in the heat
of the forge
I remember his face
as that of a man
masked by invisible night
a fire gone out in the flesh
like the flight of dead sparks
that burnt themselves black
as a beard at the end of the day
his forearms both singed of their hair
and his hands held hard as old iron
forked in the bone
with a hissing of nails
bitten down to the quick
surely
he'd a reason for rising …

I'd heard

for the want of a nail
the horse went unshod
for the want of a horse
the battle was lost

and I loved Pip more for his kind-hearted
Joe Gargery and
the one-handed farrier
had status at the fair barn
for being an expert of quarter cracks
and the soothing he gave to the spavined mare
and I with my ancestor's
smithy in Morpeth
where Lampman came of age
a mile north of the blue eye of the lake

and in the lowland
in the hollow of the field
where the tractor
sank on its wheels
if you worked the land early
its engine housed like a hog belly
caked in dry mud
sunk to the eyes in the hollow

but what is it worth
to remember
the skill in a craft long to learn
like the poets of war
when time is a child with a gun

Unimportant Work

I learned there's always unimportant work to do
and sometimes it begins in the morning of the last day
and sometimes on the first morning of the next

JBL

after my uncle's back got bad
we hired a man
to shear the sheep and
as my mother complained
when the men came into the house
from their work at the barn
the men who sat at her table
never had a word
for the woman who served
the meal — as she drifted about
like steam over heat

the sheep shearer bent over the well-fleeced ewe
lifted and set her on her dock
bleating and waving her legs
like a beetle on its back
as he calmed her
with the surety and confidence
of his chattering hand
her wool falling away
like a shrugged coat
and winter went that way
into spring
as with the shivering sheep
and the rains of early April
turned the meadows green
with a blushing of grass

and the dumb dog
hid in a hole in the hay
or under the baler
in the dark cave of the implement shed
his eyes
blinking out from that
grotto in the earth beneath deep machinery
and *a dog*
should at least be as
smart as his master
my father said
knowing full well
that this particular dog
had come from the sheep shearer's
whelp as a pup
and everyone referred to him as
'the retard'

and I said
uncle, hide all your valuables
under the baler
or there by the silo
where he hides among feed sacks
and cut hay

he being the last dog
on the farm
just before all the sheep
were sold for dreaming

The Rope Maker's Imaginings

what need he care
for the depth of the well
or the scale of the wall
his is not
the hangman's burden to bear
nor has he a thought for the strength of the bull
nor the pull of the shark
in the burning palms of the sea

dear Gordius
with your thoughtful knots

dear Tantalus
and your mindful thirst

there's a ledge somewhere
for a tethered scream
and a wished-for death
like the wind that haunts a howling crag
all Sirens mad with lust

what waits
for the hawser's hands
to give
what it means in the dark
it also holds in the light
as it drops
from the sky
to a wave

given slack or cut
it slips
and releases the levering hay

my mind
might gather it back
like a spool
and measure each yard
to the field
as the field is measured in seed

go catch me a crop
in a farmer's palm

or the earth
in an ocean of sail

I'll tell you
the rope makers dream of this

and if there's a coil
like a viper's nest
or a blunt podge
soaked in tar
there's never enough
in a middle's worth
nor an end
too close to the last

In the Days of the Fuller Brush Man

in the days of my youth
when the home
was a housewife's world
when the bread man and
the milkman and the Fuller Brush man
came calling
when women were mothers
and mothers wore aprons all day
as they answered
the knock at the door
drying their hands on a towel and
fixing their hair with the sweep of a finger
as they walked - I remember
the fly sticker mornings
hung in humbug colours
some still buzzing
and busy with the dying of flies
how they resembled
unspent shotgun shells
before the uncapping and stretching
still sticky and sweet
with rumours of blooming
pulled open and thumbtacked
to the lintels
as sometimes they'd catch
a wayward moth
still flexing its wings and taking a breath
like a brooch in a closet

and oh - there were jokes
about children
sired by the carload
jokes about the farmer's
prettiest blue-eyed daughter
rolling her hips in her ginghams
like the turning over of oats

and then
with the catalogue strangers
and then
with the glass-bottle dangers
a cream line horizon
like stocking-top stays
when I was a Wonder Bread boy
in PF Flyers
bolting green in the shins from wet grass

my mother considering growth lines
with pins in her mouth
her daughter, my sister
on top of a chair as a ladder
her hem let out at the knee

when the summer
was melting the butter
like a flame that shortens a candle
and the sunlight
was drying the hay

In the Arc Welder's Blinding Light

don't look
my father said
of the arc welder's work at the local garage

and I saw him there
clad like an Arthurian knight
complete in helmet and visor
touching metal to metal
with a brilliant flash
of silver light
blooming in his hand
not the dancing sparks
of a grinder
nor the shaken singe
of a branch drawn burning from fire

more like the trace of creation
passing between God
and Adam
a luminous white
revelation
like sheet lightning over the lake
and seeing however briefly a glimpse of the far American shore

there are stories
of foolish children
wistfully watching
the black rim of a solar eclipse

of Lot's wife
her body sculpted in salt

of soldiers come home from the wars
so wounded in the mind
that the world they once knew
went suddenly dark
as though they stood in a cave locked deep in the earth

of red measles with daylight
slithering in
under the pulled-down
window blind
seeking to steal the sick heat of the boy in the fever room

and it was all of us living
for that 'don't look'
moment
when the Sirens begin to sing
when the nest of vipers
flickering their tongues
in Medusa's hissing scalp
fall still

and you can't look away
from the consequence of stone

or poor doomed
Eurydice slipping out of reach
like a wisp of smoke
whispering as it vanishes
like a voice
you can't hear, though it's clear that the voice is your own

The Night Soil Man

there's a story
an elderly friend
would tell
concerning the occasion
when the night soil man
in his cups
bent over the privy hole
accidentally
ejected his dentures
as with a splash
the upper plate bit
into the filthy effluent
and sank
out of sight in the fly worry
of a summer evening
and he was too drunk at the time
for the bother
it would wait until morning
when sunrise at dawn
broke at the edge
of the lake
burning over the purified blue
bleaching the day waves
and so
he came with a hook
on a line
gone grappling
in the blackened splash
of a lead weight plunging through
other people's biology
until with an expert
jigging he drew forth
the half-smile
and dipping that pink-and-white

prosthetic into a pail
with a rinse and a swish
like washing the grit from a wound
he popped them
back where they'd come from
and then
lining the seat
with the news of the day
gave a common meaning
to us all

that comic tale
told round a cottage fire
shedding sparks in the night air
that lesson in biology
made me think of the time
my mother
worried over her black stool
showed her son
the charcoal-coloured
unflushed waste
asking me — *am I dying*

what answer might I give
to the woman
who gave me her breast
who washed
my soiled diapers
hung bleached on the laundry line
trailing their shadows
like ghost sails of ships anchored in the wind
the woman who came full circle
as we all do
being human ...

Home Guard

during the war
my maternal grandfather
was appointed
as one of the on-guard
citizens, who
given over to the practiced soldiering
of the local amateur
must have set out into the night
with lantern
donning the tin-pot helmet
of the Anglo-Canadian army
the one that looked for all
like an overturned shaving bowl
the hard bubble on the skull
and the broad brim flaring out from the brow
leather straps flapping like earlocks
and I imagine him there
torching the shadows
for fear of the presence of spies
hiding like tomcats
in crawl spaces
all along the line
to Mull Crossing
where night train saboteurs
slept like fog in the ditches
with a slow responding of accented English
and book-learned idioms
those come-out-of-hiding
lovers caught in moonlit assignation
fighting death with sex in combat zones

and he had
daughters at home
my mother among them
and a wife
stoking the cookstove
at four in the morning
for want of the tea
when he came home looking for comfort

and how to remember
with any conviction
the truth in the peril
so far from the front
so distant in time since then
when Harry Busteed
came in and away from the danger
that lurked in the fencerows
with cows lonesome lowing
and birdsong announcing the day

The Milkman's Epiphany

the nonagenarian milkman
came into the museum
with the idea of donating a few photographs
from when he and his horse-drawn wagon
had plodded through the city
clip-clopping among houses
dropping off ultra-white soft-stoppered bowling-pin bottles
and gathering empties in a glassy clang
come along the streets
in the catcall of small porches with big doors
when women wore aprons all day
and the warm cows lowed in the stanchion
sawing their bolus
and taking the self-assured hands
of the men who were hired to milk them
in summer the children could taste the grass in the lactose
in winter the grain-sweetened cream
and everywhere was once upon an ever whenever it was ever thus

and the milkman told us both
how he'd worked on a farm in his youth
before the thirty year stint until he was the last of his kind
in the city
how he'd been orphaned in England
shipped overseas by Barnardo
the doctor with a benevolent idea of what to do
with the clapperdudgeons of London
how the first man he'd worked for was a cruel bastard
the proof being he didn't even give him a day off at Christmas
the docent spoke up ... *you know he was a strict Presbyterian*
and neither he nor any of his clan celebrated Christmas
they didn't believe in birthdays
and it was a moment, like turning up the lamp
in a blind man's house
all the truth was in the shadows
and what he hadn't seen he still didn't see
and what he saw most clearly wasn't there at all

Elevator Girl

it's hard to resist
making a salacious joke
about the lifelong occupation
of the woman
who for almost thirty-five years
operated the Otis-Fensom elevator
at Kingsmill's Dry Goods Store
on Dundas Street in London, Ontario
indeed, there's something
heroic to be said
of someone who
with the expertise of Phileas Fogg
could find level floating
with the floor lever
of the lift
easing it down
so the lips of the sill
met as though for a kiss
and so you might
glide without worry of tripping
and then
there were the brass
scissor doors to consider
and of course
the needfulness of bells
chiming the presence
of someone waiting somewhere
like a ghost imagining levitation

you'd make little boys
titter behind their hands
to hear you utter the words *Ladies Lingerie*
as they tumbled out
the door delightfully informed
by mothers with naughty children
dragged beyond the hoistway
into the glamour
of mannequins in black brassieres

and of course
a director of blue movies
has made a film called *Elevator Girl*
about a nymphomaniac
who fantasized all day
behind a shy smile

but that wasn't you — no
you wore sensible shoes
and a smart frock
fighting off ennui
behind your smile
making chitchat with shopping strangers

while only you knew your husband
waiting at home
had been destroyed by the war
five years in a Stalag
starved on grass soup
under a sky
which even then
was sometimes shining and blue
as the best-fired china in Dresden

The Carpenter's Apprentice

for Harry Busteed

my mother's father
knelt at his bedside
in nightly devotion
as a farmer might
kneel in a field
with that bend of the knee
for testing the friable clay
in the spirit of spring and
he was a good man
in this common devotion
saying his prayers
in the quiet
like the doing of devoirs
when God was in His heaven
like the dropping of rain
that sweetens the earth in a drought
and for me
he was a man from whom
a boy might learn
his lessons

spit on the nails
let the saw do the cutting
the hammer
the hammering and
measure twice, cut once

in this these carpenter's homilies
for the building of houses as homes
when the walls invisible
rise like girders of smoke
and lintels of string
snapped blue

find plumb and be true

where the line of the land in the far
holds the sun
in the dawn and at dusk
and the lake
is divining the moon
like a watering stain in pure silk

what's a burden to bear
when what's buoyant
is love
like the inbreath
tugging the buttons and
lifting the shirt at the nape
or the breeze in the orchard
where peaches in pairs
take heart
as they swell and then blush
before falling

what happens to all
as we rise
from the bedside by dreaming
when the lifeline
is pressing the pillow
with all of your children
grown old

The Carpenter's Afterlife

for Robert Priest after his poem "Give Us a Floor"

there is a story my grandfather tells
of the day
the entire funeral fell through when the floor gave way
like thin ice under a village full of hometown skaters
and there was a great
groaning of the house
for want of a wake in the basement
for the tears of woe in the cellar
with women wailing
in rubble and men
thrashing through wreckage as though
gripping at flotsam in deep water
a floating dry-soak of sunken boards
and broken-hearted joists
snapped oak
and a storm in the hundred-year forest
what the underworld wants
of the quick-witted swimmers of earth
stroking the dust
as it is with black-veiled walkers
in the spidery darkness of a web-smoky crawl space
the mourners
with sorrow weeping in the architecture
for their loss of faith
in the old carpenter
a single nail smouldering in his mouth
the burning head
the ashen irony of rust
and the floor's true intention

Advice from My Grandfather

... never curl your thumb
or close your hand round the crank
when you're starting the tractor, boy
or she'll kick like a mule
with a twist of your wrist
that will crack the fine bone
for the marrow
turning your arm in its sleeve
like wringing the water
from a wet rag ...

but my grandfather
who was
brilliantly unmechanical
made a fist in his youth
and the engine rolled backwards
the force of it slinking up his arm
to the shoulder
like the slipping of rope
through a ring
and his radius splintered
like a dry stick
or the sharp report
of saltpeter touched by a hot match
right where the button turned up
at the cuff

and I remember the knob in the bone
just where the tatterdemalion fabric
of his long johns ended
worn even in summer
with the frayed circumference of obvious flannel

and I remember the police braces
holding the grey O of his trousers
up to the umbilicus he was born with
and I remember the black felt boots
and the hooded lids of his old-eyed face
blinking in wonder
with the fascinating click and tongued snick
of his dentures
slipping out his mouth
for the proof of a smile

never leave her in gear
when you crank
or she'll jump on her wheels
like a horse that remembers the field
with the aching of winter for spring

and he watched
while I grappled with work
having a care for my loose-fingered hand
giving the engine its meaning
when the first spark caught in the gas

The Casket Maker's House

he tells me
that where he lives
was the old location
of the casket maker's house
a hundred years ago
since when he fashioned
every funerary box
for the dying in the town
now haunted by Halloween
a pyramid of pumpkins
a thousand gauzy ghosts
draping the skeletal branches of the lawns
in decorative rags
like Spanish moss or
cobwebs in a hiding hole
faux markers for the dead
undead three seasons
in a storage shed
last night the hunter's moon
lit up the spirit of a passing mist
like something seen
through fathoms lit within
by sunken lamps
held in a drowning sailor's grip
gone down and down and fading
where dwelt the denizens
that blink at hooks
and dropping anchors
stirring bottom silts like waking souls

I hear a hammer
and an audible saw
I hear
a sobbing hand that holds
with morbid carpentry
the measuring out of every local life
oh yes, we've lived through apple cider scented days
while jack-o-lanterns grinned
like schadenfreude in a ghoulish gourd
the undertaker in his wooden suit
prepares the slatted cerements
for centuries of somber sleep

The Grass Cutter's Kindness

someone has set a white
ten-gallon pail
turned over as you would
to sit
and take a rest
for a quiet palaver
on a long morning
in the meadow, just off
the trail
the sort of short-stack
permission you give yourself
when you're not quite
tired enough to stop, though you stop
in any event
whenever the urgency subsides
and enters into the warm lacuna
of a conversation
concerning the want of rain
in a dry month
or sunshine that melts
the glint from hail

and as you approach
the vacant stool
you see her
the killdeer on her nest
in the sheltering shadow
of that hollow bucket
and it occurs to you
that she is nesting there
having laid her eggs
in the small circumference
of gravel
rounded up in a circle
swelling out of the earth
like an inbreath of stone

and you realize that this
is a grass cutter's kindness
meant to keep her safe
as he yaws through the thickening green
as a boat might
among rocks, or a
farmer a stump
or as you would
in Havana, have a care
for the broken sidewalks
of the Malecón

and just for a moment
she moves
lifting her feathered breast
and you glimpse
what she guards
spackled eggs among speckled stones

and if there isn't a God
there should be
where life is concerned
with life and she sees you
and forgives you for this lapse in faith

The House Painter's Male Gaze

how under blue heaven could he help but
stand accused
of the male gaze
the masculine gawk, the manly leer, the
ineluctable ogling of his gender in lust
as he clattered up
the ladder going rung by rung
to the lip of the roof
arriving there on the last instep dowel, the struts
of his lifting thrust toward heaven
and leaning into the bent tin of the eave
where it dimpled with the weight of him
like thumb-bruised fruit
and there to find the soft rot
of old lumber
the stained soffit over-ripened by time
spent raw in the rain
the rusted nailheads
half pulled like the exoskeletons
of wood wasps waggling in
and easing out
as though arriving at or leaving from
the hot hive humming in the attic wall
that memory of hammer strike
stinging the side of the house
where the once-upon-a-time carpenter's blow
slipped and missed

but the homeowner's sexy daughter
sunbathing in the yard
stretched out in the green hammock of the earth
lolling there like a creature of light
with him
dipping his brush in the white skim
reaching through the thick circumference
responding to his touch like cream on milk
and there
in the wet shine of the fascia
there on the crimped curl
of the gutter
he stroked brilliance with the bristles
flexing and waving farewell to old weather
bidding adieu to the rust left weeping in the grain

while she in the yard rolled
on her hip in the dew
her shadow cast in the wind-rippled moiré of the grass
like the crossing of cloud
in that what-are-you-looking-at light
where her body fell out of the sky

The Toothpaste Tester's Yellow Grin

my friend, the chemist,
told me that when he was young
his first employment
involved that of being
a *toothpaste tester*
and he smiled
and to this day, he said
he cannot stand the smell
of peppermint
showing me a mouth of teeth
stained the colour
of a smoker's piano
old ivories particulate
with remnants of breakfast
little rag ends of meat
clinging like button threads
and the hard-to-see molars
laughing backwards
deep in the coal seam
beyond the thin vermilion border
where the light must
carry itself
as it does in the lamp harp
of a linen shade smouldering bright
even when a blind man
has a good idea
concerning nightfall

and that was his young work
and the shadow of its long result
to be so mentholated
by the taste of time
the black mirror flavour
of anise and licorice root
wagging in the gums
like frost in a tombstone

what's lost by *because*
at the root of the story
goes missing that way
in everyone's life

what can't be seen and
isn't seen
is there in the thinking and the
dreaming

Goddamned Dentists

"… goddamned dentists don't know nothin' …"
the words of Thomas Shiel Malott spoken in the field
while smashing his false teeth with a stone

Doc McCutcheon's
dark little torture chamber
whined with the sound of
water-cooled drills
where the air stunk of
burning bone
and teeth flew
like shards of china
splintering along the crack lines
of a gilded cup

rather a string, a doorknob
and a good quick slam
that rapid extraction
for the pillowslip fairy
where the tooth
vanished in the dark
with a blink and a swallow
like sweet anise sucked down
to a white pebble of hard candy

in the morning
the bluenose shining silver sailed
in slight relief
for the purchase
of a gap-smile dreamer

she came and went
in a wing's blur
a single breath
so small a sigh in time
her palm a pebble dap
that skips on stillness
when the stillness barely stirs
the pulse points
in the deepest regions of the night

oh do not bother
to fear
the little man in granny glasses
crossing the room
in your direction
where you sit, a child
in a jacked-up chair
your head tilted back, mouth
kited open
like an old man sleeping

he's a ghost now
and the fog in the faith of his life has lifted

it's your mother
who slipped from the room
with your tooth in her hand

and your father
who ferried the dime

The TV Repairman

the TV
repairman
comes to the house on the farm
he kneels
by the set like a priest
watching the snow on the screen
and then
the storm begins to roll
in horizontal waves
like the shadows of light
in the rippling slats
of a wind-stirred
venetian blind and
then it ripples
with static and swirls
like grease in grey water
he fiddles
a single screw
and then
wiggles a tube
with a schurring of sparks
from an age of the Marlborough Man
and zoftig women
in movies
one foot on the floor
tomfoolery in the bed
when murder was bland
and men died
in bloodless wars
or were shot from the saddle in harvests of death
as they fell from their horses
to dust like the wheat that falls to the scythe

and there he was
with his case of cathodes
while fuses
blew in the box
and lights died down to the wick

and the world
came into the parlour
with a twitching
of weather on an overcast window
sleeting the screen

with mother
doing her housedress calisthenics
fanny bump-bump-bump bump bump
fanny bump-bump bump-bump bump
and a test pattern at midnight
and a warning of nuclear winter
come by way
of America ...
where all we had to fear
gathered on the border of time
like an eagle
with the earth in its talons

but then the next day
it was a Howdy Doody
morning of breakfast cereal roosters
returning with a romper room
magical mirror guessing at names in the room and
the man with big pockets
and a moustache
like a clothing brush on his upper lip
and only
thirty minutes at six o'clock

for the world at large to reveal itself
to the farm and
to the village
where for the boy at home
it was winter manure
lacing the snow
while the straw mow
shrank to a cat's nest
a mewling of claws and blind hunger
and the grain
blinked to dust on the floor

the TV repairman
closing his case with a satisfied click
as the cities
came clear
as the cleaning of windows
with pantomime palms

see your breath on the glass
how it glows

Like Wordsworth I Find
Myself Composing as I Walk

consider if you wish or if you will
the ochre palms
of the butcher's daughter
who smiles to offer up
the heart of the beast
like the crimson organ of a saint
set out
in shining paper
waxed one side
know this - her story
involves sharp knives and saws
no clowns or cartoon kings
sufficient to the truth
there's only one of these per death
the farm wife
cooks it rich and stuffed with bread
and she's the hunter's hero
old shaman fires
cast their smouldering shadows on her face

as though
no one has ever gone before
I'm set a single task
to solve the small confusions
of a single life

the lovers
in their veils of ash
the dragons
dying in dark storms
that last a hundred thousand years
all lava rivers racing for the sea
tsunamis rising in an island sky
blue touching blue
the grain
that floods the nostrils
of a drowning child

a poet told me yesterday
a fish is not aware
that it is surrounded by water …

until it isn't   I reply

I've seen them
gasping their gills on land
or writhing
sounding the tin bottom
in the shallow puddles of a boat

if God is not
the mountainous stone that
struck the earth from space
now lying in the belly of the gulf
then how is he
the pebble in the shepherd's sling
the guided hand
whose sword struck darkness
in the giant's mind

who sets the poet
singing on his throne

is also he
who steals the general's wife

The Men Who Worked at the Mill

we were talking
of how smooth the boards
on the floor
of the local mill
how like walking on
nailed satin in silk-slipper feet
and those mill men with faces
powdered in white grist
like gulal dusted
from monochromatic celebration
of the local harvest
where the great rustic engines
of the tall wooden towers
were grinding the annual glean
and one of us
recalled how the chop
was caught in a burlap sack
and then tied with a knot
he'd forgotten
a simple un-Gordian thing
a farmer might solve with a flick of the wrist
loosening quick as the hunger of hogs
that run from the straw to the trough

I remember how
those mill men would stand
blowing leisurely smoke
from filter free fags
burned down to the nicotine nubs
of quick-bitten hands
there where the ghost webs
blew in like cat whiskered gauze
caught full as it is with the gothic dust
that gathers in lace

and one of those fellows
who thought me a fool
to be young
intending to teach me a game
he called 52-card pickup
without pause ruffling a pack of cards
so they flew from his hands
in the air
how many fluttering hearts
how many knaves
how many jacks in the corner
how many spades on the ground

Casanova's Barnyard

tomcats, bulls, boars
roosters, buck rams, billy goats
with their
chin whiskers like Fu Manchu
like Freud, like certain fuzzy-faced civil war generals
these being big ideas of the barnyard
bellowing and grunting and yowling and
bleating and crowing
think here of the raw-cocked dog sniffing the wind and
humping the musk of otherwise seemingly empty air
as though for a warning of rain

the drake quacking
and flacking his clipped wings
in the dust he stirs under the truck

the great wide zoological
saturnalia of the sheepfold
like dry earth greening under
a cloudburst and then ...
on the feed sack
the feline conceiving
a brief blindness, a sightless desire with
a thirst for milk in the lambing, milk in the calving
milk in the whelping, and farrowing
where the sow lies weeping white sorrow

and what of the hatching
what of the tooth that breaks the shell
who candles the eggs in the henhouse

come here then
sit down by me
here on this redolent bale
this fading, this etiolating and fragrant summer
there are moments without you
I'm touching with the palm of my soul
like the heat that you leave
on a chair

The Undertaker's Tell

Never treat a woman with disrespect.
Never bring the police to my door.
And never
play poker with an undertaker.
            George Lee's advice to his son

"...an effortless repudiation of the whole shebang"
            Don McKay from his poem "Adagio for a
Fallen Sparrow"

    (the mortician's smile
    his only tell
    concealed
    a winning sorrow)

in his hand he held
the knave of hearts, his axe
in profile
flushed to the thin moustache
and gripping a feather
in a pinch and
never had he seemed so close
to raking in the coin
for there
in the embers of a final *see*
resides the rubric
the hot red memory of fire
like breath on ash
in a columbarium of mindful flame
excitable as the soul like a seed in soil
though blind as the living earth in germination
given over to the greening of the weedy end row
after rain ...

and he can't believe his luck
for here's a man whose
house is full
as any funeral
and there's a fellow who knows four sevens
make a month of Sundays
and there as well
the gravedigger
clutches five spades that make a whole

go bury the dead man's hand
the joker's gone wild
in the pack
he's such a card
his laughing palm his ringing hat
for the seventh life on the dying cat

The Gravedigger as a Child

how many graves have I dug
in my day
standing the spade in the clay
cutting the flesh of the earth
where the sod
comes away like the soft
green peel
of the hide of a beast

a boy with a thought
for what he must bury
a mouse, a cat, a
matchbox bird, a runt
a calf, a lamb, the
heartache of a morning
when the dog soul
lifted its nose at the moon
and in that white silence
gave way to the quiet
as mist gives way to the sun
with a gentle surrender of evaporate darkness

next come the difficulties
tree roots
refusing the face of the spade
where they thrust through the edge
of the hole
like the arm of a child
too real in the bone
for the ghost work it's doing

then you strike stone
blunting the frost
where it floats
with fertile erosion
of glacial rivers of time

and then
in the seep hollows
you come to collapsing
where even
the dry summer weeps
and the wet soil melts into sand

and how
as you seal it all in
like the seed of a dream
the chthonic sorrows
sob at your feet
with a wish to climb out
where the dead thing
drops in
with a sad splash and
an airless sigh

The Man from Darling in Chatham

the day
the man from Darling came to the farm
he drove in a flatbed stake truck
rumbling back the lane to the field
where the night before
the cow had been struck dead
by lightning
she'd taken shelter
under the elm that stood
smouldering in the morning
with smoke in the branches
like the drifting through and away of fog

and she was stiff
in the body
and left there
by the touch of the God of creation
His thunderbolt
shocking her lifeless
as she grazed
on the singed-black grasses of heaven

the man from Darling simply
took her away
as he did
another day
come for the old ewe
who'd died on her back
in a ditch
her legs flipped to the sky
as she'd struggled to breathe
with the evening gone into the night
for the wanting of darkness we share
when we're slipping away in the ether
like forms newly lost in the gloaming
and oaks that vanish at dusk

and then, what of the bull
who'd straddled the fence
as he bellowed alone
till he broke at the girth with his ribs
like a branch snapped over the knee

and sometimes the work that we do
is the work
of the man from the town

if you come to the city
there where the dead cattle burn
for the fat on the flesh
and the glue in the bone
you might
take in breath with its stench of belief

what began in the womb
like a spark in dry grass
came to catch in the ditches
and level the barns
and burn the most holy cathedrals of home
where we kneel in the flames
shaping fire

The Work a Boy Can Do

two years after we moved
into the big house on the farm
with my grandmother
ailing beyond chores
her body softening with illness
her flesh like baked fruit
and I turned five
learning a first death
as it is with ash that cools
when the fire greys into powder
and then
as with wind in the brazier
one life is gone from the house to the land
and my grandfather's bed
went one-side cold
entering the dark moon of a marriage
when a widower's mind
is given over to heartache
and sorrowful dreaming

all of it well beyond me
though other than mourning there were
jobs a boy could do
involving carrying the milk
from the barn to the house
with an ache in strength
and the handle-hurt
from the ring on the pail that bites
into the palm
and the set down, set down, set down
the resting in gravel
the resting in grass
with the hoop circle
where you leave a fascinating green crush
and the refusal to surrender
your young muscles straining
like a feckless marionette

the spider silk of the will webbed to blue heaven
and your mother waits in the kitchen
watching the sun yellow eye of summer
blinking in time like butter in the buttermilk

and also the egg gather
how warm they were
brown-shelled and lovely
fresh from the nest
stolen from under
hen bellies brooding
those red-feathered fowl
their voices clucking softly
like children talking in a sleepy darkness

and there's death yet to do its work
its shovel foot stepping above a grave to dig
like the push of fog
against an earthen floor
seeking a breathing window, seeking an open door

Being the Doctor

the Christmas I received
the doctor's kit
those medical instruments
waiting in the pine scent
of the farm parlour
held within the rattle of a faux case
with its plastic hasp
unfastened with a satisfactory snap
like the sound
of a wishbone breaking dry

and there you were
with the heat of heavy blankets
cast aside for the house call
lying in wait
in the guest bed
your body fevered
by the first moments
after waking ...

and you surrendered
your heart to the movement
of the small bell of the stethoscope
as I listened

following the pulse points downward
to the last loosening

In the Gardens of Sorrow

whenever we followed
familiar roads
with my father at the wheel
our journey
to the city on the Thames
was ever much like the fluvial meander
of the flowing there
of a gentle river
our headlamps proving
the darkness as real
with an amber glow
flooding the grey shoulders
like the dragging of silk over gravel
or when moonlight
crosses still water and
every journey
involved his voice
like an audio loop
as though we were learning
the way of the lost
and we were not his children
but the elder-nursed
or the bell-at-the-door
slow dog waking
and then came the last turn
in the pencil-maze
of our going - he'd
always say
by way of reminder
that is where
the Mibs Caramel Crisp man
lives - as there
in the sweet air
as if when

you rolled down your window to listen
you might hear
the gunshot popping
of fairground confection
followed by the sticky dippering
of honey-coloured light

and it was a small house
set among many
in a world of oceans
and starlight
with a footstep on the moon
and the satellites of Saturn
and the great wide sweep
of the Milky Way
and to think then of a young boy
as the fixed point
of consciousness
listening to the voice of his father
that drift of words like the wind in an elm
and the echo there
of sweet explosions
that hot little bang
and everything subsiding
into melancholy recollection
and wishful repetition
in the gardens of sorrow we've come to

Ode on a Toy Rifle

I wonder at the whereabouts
of the toy rifle
my uncle made for me
all those many years ago
working away
in the tool shed on the farm
first carving
a three-foot two-by-four
shaping it into
a gunstock, then
drilling a hole and
inserting a length of pipe
with a plumber's perfection
that faux barrel exactly
the right size for a boy's ballistics
then a fine screw threaded in
as a front sight
and fashioning a trigger guard
from a bent spoon
hammered into a perfect form
so it fit the stock exactly
like a leaf you might curl in your palm
to catch a thirst for rain
and then
the carry strap cut from mossy horse halter
so there it was
from butt to bore
something to put to the purpose
of imaginary war

and for five years
I soldiered
the dangerous borderline of the cow pasture
in that lustrum of wonder
till childhood subsided
into the AWOL of adolescence
and I left behind a life of dreams
that abandoned rifle leaning somewhere
like an October cornstalk
wintering into cold weather

and has it vanished, yes
has it been burned
as broken things
are often burned, perhaps

but I am still
burdened by the fardel of a need
for thankfulness

what swelling rivers
have to say
in gratitude about the gravity of rain
or streams
that wind through crooks of land
meandering to cool the lake
arriving where the memory of snow
might lift a pebble in the chill
or stir a shell or roll a blur of sand
or send a shoal of minnows
in a silver swirl
like a casting of coin
when wishing falls away
like sediment in clarity of silt

Lazy Eye

it was suggested by a scholar
that the greatest invention
in human history
is the *lens*
and I learned while listening
that the father of optics
was an Arab mathematician
name Alhazen who lived
a thousand years ago
during the golden age of Islam
and who experimented
in a darkened room
with light from a pinhole
revealing the inverted image of
the first camera obscura

and in that I was born
on the anniversary
of the birth of the lens grinder Spinoza
I learn a new thing every day …

and in that
I acquired my first spectacles
at age eight
for correcting an affliction
the optometrist identified as
lazy eye

I sometimes think of the Romans
with their reading stones
magnifying the text
as they slid
the beryl over the words
on the page
thereby making the language *pop*
like a whisper suddenly clarified
by being surrounded by silence

and I remember
punishing myself
by removing my spectacles
and dragging them
lens down over the desk
scratching the glass
so from then on until forever
the world of my childhood
seemed like something
seen as scraped raw with everything
etched in a boy's stupid rage
like the rain streaked windows
on the filthy glass at the barn

and if I dreamed as I did once in the deserts of Wadi Rum
upon seeing the crusaders' castle standing
as a remnant of holy wars
revealing a mirage of sand-swept spirits
wind-whipped dust devils like soldiers of the cross
half alive in the come to life dying of weather

meanwhile I broke pencils
struggling with grade nine algebra
while everywhere around my desk
ghosts swept and swirled
like the white silk robes of Peter O'Toole

What Happened to My Brain of Youth

… it was the winter I stopped warring
as I dropped my sword forever and
removed my Roman greaves
gave up the siege of Stalingrad
those broken bodies fallen
in a blizzard swimming snow
no more Achilles dreaming
in his tent
I set aside
my musket, my shako, and my scarlet coat
and so my officer's gorget
became a man's medallion
my muzzle for a vase
a blooming rose of smoke
the cowboy rowels
spun till they were still
like whirling wind toys in a dying off of storm
my mufti gone to moths

what happened
to my brain of youth

imaginary hoodoos swept away to dust
as I exchanged a cockhorse
for a broom's guitar
my citadel, my palisade
my fortress with each timber fallen
like the rotting castles on the shoreline of wet sand
the Valkyries of sorrow
sang as lake gulls sing landing on a wave
when Helen's beauty sank and swelled
upon a bridal bower
old Agamemnon's empty ships
left rocking on the tides of burning Troy

meanwhile the myrmidons of all grandfather death
whisked through the cobwebs
like a fletch of Cupid's arrows
over Agincourt's demise
to thrill the silver-breasted
lovers of the flowers of light
a feathering
like reed shafts with ornamental nocks
and roots
that reeve the armour of the human heart
like wishes on a whispering of candle flame

what happened
to my brain of youth

my helmet on the floor
beside the bed
strap-shadowed to a ghost
someone I knew
and know no more

The Work that We Do

my high school friend and I
were hired by his father
for the dipping of lumber
in Paris green
as from a long trough of liquefied arsenic
we drew
the stained weep
of the kiln-cured pine
so the knots went dark
as grass in cloth
small swirls
like the sweet genuflection
of careless children
come home with a problem
for mother to solve
that toxic heartache
of washing to do
that mischief in timber
that measure
like paint in the scantling

and we wore
gloves made of rubber
yellow gloves
long in the wrist
our thin arms
roostering in the pea gravel
of the day
the pile to the left
and the pile
to the right
one comes close to the floor
the other
climbing to the rafters as it dried

like two men on a saw
with its teeth
in the forest
two young bucks
dimming the shade
so it fell on itself
like the great sweep
of a giant clock hand

what wall in what house
hides its frame
in the plaster
what floor
holds its flooring
humming under footfalls
of whispering slippers

it's scaffolding
that dreams of the woodlot

like the acorn
spending the span of its shadow
with an axe in the cradle
and the sun in the clearing

it's the work
that we do
coming into the world

The Fossil Finder's Father

every day for several summers
living on the cliff
overlooking Long Point Bay
since before the water rose
flooding the shore
and wave-lashing the breakwall
when we would walk
the dry-foot sand
both east and west
where the crags are rubbled by boulders
I would stroll
like a man with troubles
though it wasn't that I was
bothered by cares
I stooped as a sad man
must seem in his sorrows
looking for smoothed shards
of lake-rubbed glass
for the half shells
of mother of pearl mollusks
that coral coloured interior
polished keen and shining in the sun
but it was mostly
fossils I sought
and they seemed most rare
I'd find a few - one in a week
or three in a month
looking hard
for the grey relief
of some time-worried frond
some fan of life
etched in the glacial age
of mile high ice and ichthyology

and then my son came
for a visit
jaunting along
a happy-hat dreamer
returning with two pockets
filled like gold-rush pokes
stuffed to the slash of his trousers
his hands spilling
his hat crushed to the crown

oh how I admired him
how I envied
his skill

and I thought
these are the treasures
we dig for
the ones on the surface
where the heart
daps the wrist
like a bird aborning
its egg tooth of the soul
seeking the bloodline between us

and I say nothing
but everything
there's that full silence
in the temple
like the aquifer suggesting
the rains are most deep when it rains from within

Doctor Pleva's Foolish Wishes

he came to warn us all
of the foolishness
of houses
ribboning the roads
on the way out of town
like the ghost fires
of Johannesburg
leading in thin draws of darkness
smouldering away from the city
the paraffin fumes
of burning the light
so the smoke leans into the wakening nose
like gnomon shadow
marking the morning and we
fail to learn in the long shade of an early hour
though time is teaching
the body to melt in mortification
like the blushing of the heart
rising past the hyper-sternal notch
of the pulse at the throat where the collar throbs
with that crimson shame of sinning through pleasure
when the sin is fever
and the bad thoughts true
we are grown ill with the future noise of warning voices
we are melting over the roads
and draining into the streams and ditches
we are wild chicory and milkweed sorrow
the lovely apparatus of our wings flexing
as though with the appetite of dream angels
aspiring to the lofty accumulation of blue altitude
of atmospheric haze in fritillaries of furious orange
burning over the lake at sundown
and what we have learned of autumn
we have learned too late for winter
forgetful of warning we rise
like dust in the wake of great armies
even knowing we've gone the wrong way
we go, still walking widdershins
on blistered feet in vanishing shoes

The Videographer's Lament

I carry
the device from the bedroom
where my beloved lies
in wake
of her having given me my first lesson
on the making
of a video
by means of an *iPad*

and I carry myself
as though in a feint from
having spent a week in a fever
I'm crossing the room
at a cant with the screen at a tilt
as one might
carry a slender sheet
of easily broken glass

and I see
the counter ticking off the time
and so I know it's working
as I blink at my reflection
framed by the big white thumbs
of a farmer's hands
and I see that I have the look
of a tuck-tailed dog
spooked and seeking shelter
from the thunder rumble
of a black sky
come in over the lake
as I race from the room
setting the damned thing down
on my desk
where it tilts on magnification
like a vanity mirror

and so I begin
holding forth
reading from a prepared text
avoiding the word-stumble
of a barely literate child

and I am caught in focus
every old-man fold of my face
like the rolling flesh of a Shar Pei dog

every wind-wild lock of hair
every strand of it sprung loose
like the plucked up head of a late-to-rise sleeper

yet somehow I manage
to complete the task at hand
having made a two minute video

and just for a moment
in the silence when the screen goes dark
I see myself
swirling away from the light

Ode to Librarians –
a cynic's appraisal of these times

... if I were to say to you
most librarians don't read
would you become angry
indignant, outraged by
the unearned hubris
accuse me of being
orgulous - oh do we not
now live in an
anti-intellectual age
are we not steeped
in a stupefying culture where learning
is a sin of commission
where there is an insufficiency
of baskets - a scarcity
of sheltering shade
where intelligence might hide and
erudition lock up its light
in shadow like ginseng in sunshine
while like rat moles
moiling in darkness
we blink at the brilliance
where all the Google-knowing
and all the fact-shaming rule
and all the conversational competition
in the COVID lonesome era
of the information age ...
why, there's even a service
for the quick know-nothings
who leap to their feet
with a know-it-all answer
a short-cut acquaintance
with no need to consider or comprehend
what is pi? What is the speed of light?
How many toes on a six-toed cat?

as you jump to your feet
with a cell-phone solution
you might easily own the floor
like a mouse in the moonlight
or a scurry of roaches
in a world where dancers can't dance
and singers can't sing
and poets who
though they've read nothing and
know less
hold forth from the stage
in the borrowed glint
of popular thought and clichéd phrases
but oh, how sincere,
oh how 'woke' in a gender ambiguous age

and so I return
to my unopened book
and I ask of the dog at the door
or the dog on the step
what page are you on
and I look to his ear bent up and then down
for enlightenment
as he cocks his sweet head
for a selfie
and as I return the text to the shelf
from here I can see
how the librarian smiles
to think of it there
exactly where it belongs at rest in an organized heap

though the marginalia screams
like a gut-shot prayer

and the dying by which we die slowly
succeeds in hiding all that we know
from those that don't know it who think
that we wish we were them

Elegy for the Book Writer's Dog

in the midst of my sorrow
sitting by the break wall
at the lip of the bay
feeling nothing but dog loss
I am ever so briefly
visited by the fascination
of a caravan of centipedes
crawling the ferruginous rim
of rusted iron
moving west from east
this convoy of worms
these larval energies
put to the purpose of life
in refuge
like the journey of the sun
within an insect consciousness
a thousand legs
blunting their threads
in search of a silver eye
come to the blur of a dark gate
in a poor-vision world

and I wonder where they are going, and why
see where the lake
is heaving its soul
like a sad man breathing
and also where
blue heaven reveals itself
in half-hearted brush strokes
like watercolour too thin
and fading on the page where it pools
in translucent washes that follow
the hand of creation
shown through to the other side

where the mirage
of an absent oasis
awaits us
I am carried there
in that water-shadow hallucination
of cool shade and sheltering prayer palms
shouldered high on the weaving spines
of those silver-grey
and seemingly urgent inches
these silk-road camels seeking a well

so why am I thinking now
of the booksellers
in the commerce of Cuba
their volumes laid out in random libraries
on the park tables in the central square
of Holguín
why am I drawn
to consider
the kiosks along the Seine
or the open-air shops in Stratford on Avon
or the busy trade and foot traffic
at 37 Rue de la Bûcherie
with George Whitman's daughter
selling the sunlight in Paris one word at a time

all authors and all
the work they do
laid out in the street
like the guts and cogs of old machines
something easing the wind
through the pages
some bottom of the basket
life stain
remaining as truth of the blossom
truth of the candle come to the aftershadow
of the juice that has dried from the fruit

the empty notepad
is such a brave beginning
for this unkind result
this erosion of names
these absent crosses
leaving their place like Palm Sunday bookmarks
in Psalters of Easter

am I to think
that these words, this ink
these earnest intensions
and diligent destinies
locked away in these remaindered books
these graves of trees
these epitaphs
of some sentient evening
when morning came marching
out of the earth
only to vanish
like a mending thread
pulled through a tatter
in a seam that won't hold
for the wearing

Rilke's Barber

When Rilke had his hair cut
by a barber in Paris
after the barber was finished
Rilke requested a splashing
of Houbigant parfum for men ...
the indignant barber shouted
"Unbelievable!"
and to make matters worse
Rilke had left his wallet at the hotel
and the irate barber accusing him of being a shyster
a dandy, an unscrupulous cheat
Rilke protested, "But I am the poet
Rainer Maria Rilke,"
to which the barber replied
"Of course. That's what everyone says."

I was dining with friends
and I had just received the news
that I was the recipient of a thousand dollar
poetry prize.

The waiter came to the table
and my friend said to him
"This is John B. Lee, the only three time
Poet Laureate in Canada, and he has been given
a thousand dollar poetry prize for a single poem."

The waiter waved in the air
as though to shoo the flies from the fruit
and said, "I don't even know what that means,
now may I take your order."

A Short Author Bio:

In 2005 John B. Lee was inducted as Poet Laureate of Brantford in perpetuity. The same year he received the distinction of being named Honourary Life Member of The Canadian Poetry Association and The Ontario Poetry Society. In 2007 he was made a member of the Chancellor's Circle of the President's Club of McMaster University and named first recipient of the Souwesto Award for his contribution to literature in his home region of southwestern Ontario and he was named winner of the inaugural Black Moss Press Souwesto Award for his contribution to the ethos of writing in Southwestern Ontario. In 2011 he was appointed Poet Laureate of Norfolk County (2011-14) and in 2015 Honourary Poet Laureate of Norfolk County for life and in 2017 he received a Canada 150 Medal from the Federal Government of Canada for "his outstanding contribution to literary development both at home and abroad." A recipient of over eighty prestigious international awards for his writing he is winner of the $10,000 CBC Literary Award for Poetry, the only two time recipient of the People's Poetry Award, and 2006 winner of the inaugural Souwesto Orison Writing Award (University of Windsor). In 2007 he was named winner of the Winston Collins Award for Best Canadian Poem, an award he won again in 2012. He has well-over seventy books published to date and is the editor of seven anthologies including two best-selling works: That Sign of Perfection: poems and stories on the game of hockey; and Smaller Than God: words of spiritual longing. He co-edited a special issue of Windsor Review—Alice Munro: A Souwesto Celebration published in the fall of 2014. His work has appeared internationally in over 500 publications, and has been translated into French, Spanish, Korean and Chinese. He has read his work in nations all over the world including South Africa, France, Korea, Cuba, Canada and the United States. He has received letters of praise from Nelson Mandela, Desmond Tutu, Australian Poet, Les Murray, and Senator Romeo Dallaire. Called "the greatest living poet in English," by poet George Whipple, he lives in Port Dover, Ontario where he works as a full time author.

www.ingramcontent.com/pod-product-compliance
Lightning Source LLC
Chambersburg PA
CBHW031244120626
46545CB00007B/2648